How Artists See Homes

Karen Hosack

Heinemann
LIBRARY

H www.heinemann.co.uk/library

To order:
☎ Phone 44 (0) 1865 888066
🖹 Send a fax to 44 (0) 1865 314091
💻 Visit the Heinemann Bookshop at www.heinemann.co.uk/library to browse our catalogue and order online.

First published in Great Britain by Heinemann Library, Halley Court, Jordan Hill, Oxford OX2 8EJ, part of Harcourt Education.
Heinemann is a registered trademark of Harcourt Education Ltd.

Editorial: Andrew Farrow and Dan Nunn
Design: Ron Kamen and Celia Floyd
Illustrations: Jo Brooker
Picture Research: Mica Brancic and Charlotte Lippman
Production: Viv Hichens

Originated by Dot Gradations Ltd
Printed and bound in Hong Kong and China by South China Printing Company

The paper used to print this book comes from sustainable resources.

ISBN 0 431 93220 4
08 07 06 05 04
10 9 8 7 6 5 4 3 2 1

British Library Cataloguing in Publication Data

Hosack, Karen
 Homes. – (How artists see)
 1. Dwellings in art – Juvenile literature
 2. Art appreciation – Juvenile literature
 I. Title
 704.9'4964

A full catalogue record for this book is available from the British Library.

Acknowledgements
The publishers would like to thank the following for permission to reproduce photographs:

Art Archive pp. **9** (Paul Klee © DACS 2004), **20** (Bibliothèque des Arts Décoratifs, Paris / Dagli Orti); Bridgeman Art Library pp. **4** (The National Gallery, London), **15** (© ADAGP, Paris and DACS, London 2004), **18** (The Hermitage Museum, St Petersburg, Russia), **19** (Musee d'Orsay, Paris, France), **21** (Palais du Luxembourg, Paris), **24** (The National Gallery London); Corbis pp. **8**, **10**, **11** (David Glover), **23**; Mary Evans Picture Library p. **26**; The National Gallery, London pp. **14**, **16**; Ohara Museum of Art, Japan pp. **6**, **28**; Peter Evans p. **13 top**; © Salvador Dali, Gala-Salvador Dali Foundation, DACS, London 2004 p. **22**; Statens Museum for Kunst, Copenhagen p. **27**; Tate London 2004 pp. **5** (Lowry Estate), **7 top** (© Carl Andre / VAGA, New York / DACS, London 2004), **25**; Tudor Photography pp. **13 middle**, **13 bottom**, **17 x 3**, **29**.

Cover photograph (*Curious Weather* by Mark Copeland, 1999) reproduced with permission of Portal Gallery London/Bridgeman Art Library.

Every effort has been made to contact copyright holders of any material reproduced in this book. Any omissions will be rectified in subsequent printings if notice is given to the Publishers.

Contents

Words printed in bold letters, **like these**, are explained in the Glossary.

How artists see homes

An Autumn Landscape with a View of Het Steen in the Early Morning by Peter Paul Rubens, 1636

A home is a place where people live with their families. Many artists enjoy painting the places where people live. The artist Peter Rubens painted this picture showing his own home. It looks a bit like a castle! Rubens' home is set in the middle of beautiful countryside.

The painter Lowry enjoyed **sketching** the factories and workers' cottages in his hometown of Manchester. He used simple box shapes for the houses. He painted the people using line. Lowry showed how tiny the people were compared to their homes and the huge smoking chimneys.

Industrial Landscape by L. S. Lowry, 1955

Shape and tone

This artist has painted these houses using simple shapes. Notice how details like windows and doors have been left out. The artist hasn't drawn in any of the bricks or tiles on the roofs. The houses look **three-dimensional** because different **tones** have been used for each side of the shapes.

Riverside Houses by Seiji Chokai, 1954

6

Carl Andre used ordinary house bricks to make this **sculpture**. He used the simple block shapes to create a larger rectangle on the floor. Such a simple sculpture makes us look at the shape and **texture** of the materials.

Equivalent VIII by Carl Andre, 1966

Make your own three-dimensional shape

You will need:

- *a pencil*
- *a piece of paper.*

 unshaded cube

 shaded cube

Instructions:

1 Make a copy of the unshaded cube above.
2 Using a pencil, practise making different tones of grey.
3 Shade in the sides of the cube using different tones. This will make it look three-dimensional.

Shapes and patterns

Egon Schiele put lots of detail into this picture. The patterns made by the roof tiles, bricks and windows merge with the patterns made by the drying washing. The shapes of the jumpers and dresses on the washing line make us think about the people who own them. These people live in the homes in the picture.

House with Drying Laundry by Egon Schiele, 1917

Architecture Spatiale by Paul Klee, 1915

The pattern in this painting is made by the coloured squares used for the houses. It looks a bit like a **patchwork**. The painting is very flat because **tone** has not been used to show the sides of the houses. Some of the shapes are laid on top of each other. This makes the scene feel like a busy, built-up town.

Shapes and spaces

The people who design buildings are called **architects**. When architects design homes they think about the sort of things people use their houses for. The architect Le Corbusier designed homes which look like large white solid shapes. The spaces inside these shapes are huge. Le Corbusier liked the idea of rooms flowing into each other, so he did not use many inside walls or doors. This is called open-plan design.

Villa Savoye at Poissy, France, designed by Le Corbusier, 1928–29

House by Rachel Whiteread, 1993

This is a **sculpture** of a house that was designed in **Victorian** times. Many families would have lived in the house over a period of about 150 years. In 1993, the artist Rachel Whiteread filled the house with **plaster** to make a cast of the inside. After the plaster dried she took down all the outside walls. Can you see any similarities between the white shapes of this sculpture and the home on page 10?

Drawing different types of homes

In the **fifteenth century** an **architect** and painter called Leon Battista Alberti invented a useful viewfinder tool to help him draw. An artist looks through a frame like the one at the bottom of page 13, and draws what can be seen through it on to squared paper.

Make your own Alberti square

You will need:

- a piece of card approximately 12 cm x 12 cm
- a craft knife – you MUST ask an adult to help you use this
- a pencil
- black sewing cotton
- sticky tape
- a ruler.

Instructions:

1 Make the card into a frame by carefully cutting a 9 cm x 9 cm hole in the centre. You should ask an adult to help you with this.

2 Using your pencil, measure and mark 3 cm and 6 cm along each side of the hole.

3 Make a small slit in the card where you have placed the marks.

4 Cut four pieces of cotton 11 cm long.

Using your Alberti square

Instructions:

1 First draw a nine-square grid on a piece of paper. Next, hold up your Alberti square in front of a house or other building that you would like to draw. You don't need to draw whole buildings. Instead, focus on interesting areas like patterns made by bricks, or shapes made by windows and doors.

2 Copy what you can see through the frame, square by square, on to your paper grid. You should now have your finished drawing!

5 Place the ends of the cotton into the slits to make a grid of nine squares on the frame. Stick down the ends of each piece of cotton with sticky tape. You should now have your finished viewfinder.

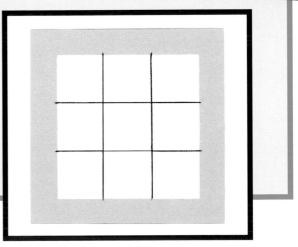

Distance and perspective

Saint Jerome in his Study by Antonello da Messina, 1475–76

The **Renaissance** was a time when lots of artists painted pictures that looked like views through a window. In this painting we are looking through a window at Saint Jerome in his study. The scene reaches far back into the room and even out through the windows in the distance. The way artists show things in the distance is called **perspective**.

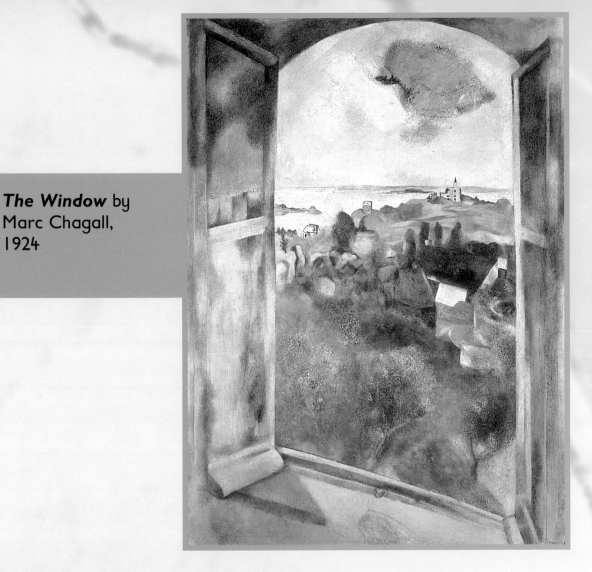

The Window by
Marc Chagall,
1924

Marc Chagall painted this scene from an upstairs
window. It looks out over some seaside houses in the
middle ground. In the background there is a
lighthouse. Because we are looking down on the
landscape from above, we can also see roof tops.
This is called a bird's eye view. Why do you think it
is called that?

Looking through doors

Everything inside this house is painted flat against the sides of the box. This even includes the furniture. When we look through the small peepholes in the sides of the box the objects look as though they are standing in a real space. It is very clever!

A Peepshow with Views of the Interior of a Dutch House by Samuel van Hoogstraten, around 1655–60

Make your own viewer

You will need:

- *scissors*
- *paint*
- *glue*
- *a pencil*
- *a rectangular cardboard box*
- *pictures of furniture cut out from magazines.*

Instructions:

1 Cut one of the box's long sides off, so you have 3 walls, a ceiling and a floor. If your box does not have a lid, you can probably just turn it on its side.

2 Paint the floor with a **chequered** pattern and the ceiling with one single colour. Next paint one side wall and the back wall with a wallpaper design. Finally, paint the other side wall with wallpaper and an open door leading through to another room.

3 Stick cut-out pictures of furniture against the walls. Overlap these slightly on to the floor and the corners of the walls. Finally, use the end of your scissors to make two peepholes, one on each side wall. You should now have your finished viewer!

Colour and mood

Harmony in Red (Red Room) by Henri Matisse, 1908–09

The colour of a room can affect how we feel when we are inside it. **Hot colours**, like red, make us feel warm. **Cold colours**, like blue, make a room feel cooler. Henri Matisse has called this painting of a red room *Harmony in Red* because the room looks so welcoming and cosy. What colour is your bedroom? How does the colour make you feel?

Vincent's Bedroom in Arles by Vincent van Gogh, about 1889

Van Gogh painted this picture of his bedroom with blue walls and orange furniture. Blue makes the room feel open and airy. The orange furniture warms the room up a bit. Blue and orange are opposite each other in the colour wheel (see panel on the right). We call these colours **complementary colours** because they help each other look brighter.

Did you know?
Yellow and purple, and green and red are also complementary colours. See how they are opposite each other on the colour wheel.

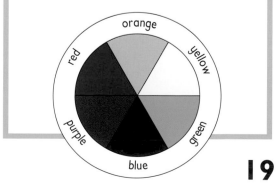

Murals

Some people like to paint pictures straight on to walls. We call these paintings **murals**. This **Roman** mural was painted on a bedroom wall over 2000 years ago. Painting a pretend view from a window would have made the room seem much larger.

Wall painting from the bedroom of a villa in a village near Pompeii, Italy, in the 1st century BC

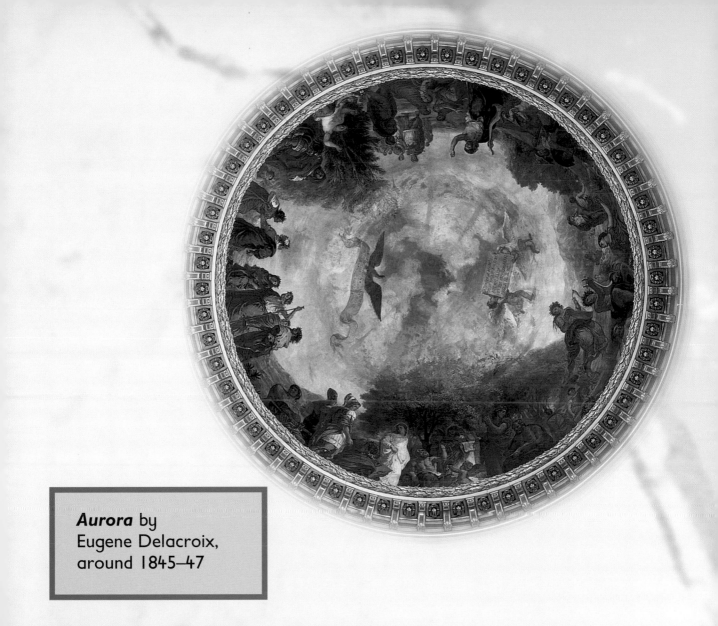

Aurora by
Eugene Delacroix,
around 1845–47

This is a ceiling mural. The artist wants us to think
that the room is very tall and open to the sky. Try to
imagine what the room would look like with such an
amazing ceiling. Do you think it would make you feel
a bit dizzy if you looked up?

21

Fantasy rooms

The artist Salvador Dali is famous for creating strange works of art. Here he has designed a room to look like a famous film star's face. The curtains are her hair. The pictures on the wall are her eyes. He has made a sofa in the shape of a pair of lips and a fireplace in the shape of her nose.

The Face of Mae West by Salvador Dali, 1934–35

Art Nouveau Interior by Alphonse Marie Mucha

Artists around the end of the **nineteenth century** were very interested in using patterns from nature in their designs. We call this style **Art Nouveau**. The fireplace in this room has been designed to look like a tree growing out of the ground. The wall is decorated with a peacock displaying its feathers.

Homes and gardens

The members of this family are enjoying being in their garden on a sunny day. The water fountain and the flower pots make the garden look very grand. The artist has painted the trees and other plants in a misty, fuzzy way. It feels as though we are watching a perfect dreamlike world.

A Lady and Gentleman with Two Girls in a Garden by Nicolas Lancret, around 1742

24

Many people have sheds at the bottom of their garden. This is where the garden tools are stored, along with lots of other things. This **sculpture** was once an ordinary garden shed. The artist has taken out all of the objects and hung them from the ceiling using transparent thread, along with bits of wood from the shed. It looks as though the shed has exploded with all the junk!

25

Tidy your room!

The objects in this room tell a story about two rich but lazy people. It is a grand room but it is a bit messy. The servant, on the right, is annoyed at having to run around after the owners of the house. Look at how William Hogarth has cleverly shown us another room through the archway. This makes the picture look more **three-dimensional**.

The Tête à Tête (The Breakfast Scene) by William Hogarth, 1745

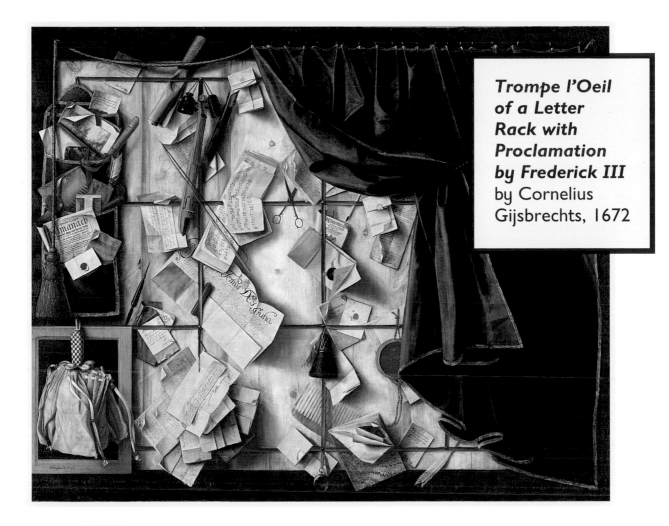

Trompe l'Oeil of a Letter Rack with Proclamation by Frederick III by Cornelius Gijsbrechts, 1672

The people in William Hogarth's picture could have done with a rack like this to keep their room tidy. The objects look so real you think you can touch them. But they are just a flat painting. We call a painted illusion like this a 'tromp l'oeil'.

Your neighbourhood

Our homes are surrounded by other homes, and the local **environment**. Robert Rauschenberg collected photographs and newspaper clippings that showed what it was like to live in his hometown. He used them to make this **collage**. We call artwork that uses lots of different materials 'mixed-media'.

A City by Robert Rauschenberg, 1962

Make your own mixed-media collage

You will need:

- *a collection of objects that remind you of your home and neighbourhood*
- *a large piece of paper*
- *some glue.*

Instructions:

1 Collect together some bits and pieces that remind you of your home and neighbourhood. These could include:

- photographs of buildings, rooms and furniture cut out from magazines
- photographs or sketches of family and friends
- printouts from the Internet about your hometown
- sweet wrappers from your local shop
- photographs or **sketches** of your local environment
- rubbings made with wax crayons showing **textures** you find near your house.

2 Arrange the objects you have found across a large piece of paper and glue them down.

3 You have now finished your mixed-media collage!

Glossary

architect someone who designs buildings

Art Nouveau style of art, architecture and design that was popular in western Europe from the 1890s to the early 1900s

chequered having a pattern of squares

cold colour colour that makes you feel cold, like blue or green

collage artwork made from materials glued on to a backing

complementary colours opposite colours in the colour wheel

environment the surroundings in which plants, animals and people live

fifteenth century period of 100 years, between 1400 and 1499

hot colour colour that makes you feel hot, like red, yellow or orange

middle ground area of a picture that is in the middle distance, between the foreground and the background

mural painting on a wall

nineteenth century period of 100 years, between 1800 and 1899

patchwork pattern made by sewing lots of small pieces of fabric together

perspective a technique that artists use to give pictures a feeling of space and distance

plaster a fine white powder that sets hard when it is mixed with water and then left to dry

Renaissance period of European history between the fourteenth and sixteenth centuries when there was a renewed interest in art

Roman from the period of the ancient Roman Empire

sculpture piece of art made from a solid material

sketch rough drawing

texture how something feels

three-dimensional when an object has height, width and depth

tone light and shade

Victorian period of history when Queen Victoria was Queen of Great Britain, from 1837 to 1901

Finding out more

More books to read

Heinemann Library's *How Artists Use* series:

- *Colour*
- *Line and Tone*
- *Pattern and Texture*

- *Perspective*
- *Shape*

Heinemann Library's *The Life and Work of* series:

- *Auguste Rodin*
- *Barbara Hepworth*
- *Buonarroti Michelangelo*
- *Claude Monet*
- *Edgar Degas*
- *Georges Seurat*
- *Henri Matisse*
- *Henry Moore*
- *Joseph Turner*

- *Leonardo Da Vinci*
- *Mary Cassatt*
- *Paul Cezanne*
- *Paul Gauguin*
- *Paul Klee*
- *Pieter Breugel*
- *Rembrandt van Rijn*
- *Vincent Van Gogh*
- *Wassily Kandinsky*

Websites to visit

www.eurogallery.org – this website lets you search the art collections of important museums and galleries across the whole of Europe.

www.nationalgallery.org.uk – this is the website of the National Gallery in London. All of the works in the collection can be seen online.

Index

Titles in the *How Artists See* series include:

Hardback   0 431 93217 4

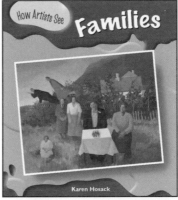

Hardback   0 431 93218 2

Hardback   0 431 93221 2

Hardback   0 431 93220 4

Hardback   0 431 93219 0

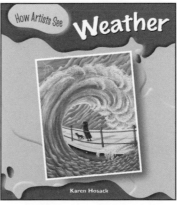

Hardback   0 431 93222 0

Find out about the other titles in this series on our website www.heinemann.co.uk/library